MEDIEVAL LIVES

Lady of the Manor

MOIRA BUTTERFIELD

W

FRANKLIN WATTS
LONDON·SYDNEY

First published in 2008 by Franklin Watts

Copyright © Franklin Watts 2008
Artwork copyright © Gillian Clements 2008

Franklin Watts
338 Euston Road
London NW1 3BH

Franklin Watts Australia
Level 17/207 Kent Street
Sydney, NSW 2000

A CIP catalogue record for this book is available
from the British Library.

Dewey number: 940.1

ISBN 978 0 7496 7740 4

Printed in China

Franklin Watts is a division of Hachette Children's
Books, an Hachette Livre UK company.

Artwork: Gillian Clements
Editor: Sarah Ridley
Editor in chief: John C. Miles
Designer: Simon Borrough
Art director: Jonathan Hair
Picture research: Diana Morris

Picture credits:
Abbaye de L'Epau Loire/Gianni Dagli Orti/The Art Archive: 41. Arquivo Nacional da Torre do Tombo Lisbon/Alfredo Dagli
Orti/The Art Archive: 24. The Art Archive: 4,16. Biblioteca d'Ajuda Libon/Gianni Dagli Orti/The Art Archive: 32. Biblioteca
Nazionale Marciana Venice/The Art Archive: 18. Bibliothèque Saint-Genieve Paris/ Bridgeman Art Library : 13. Bodleian Library
Oxford/The Art Archive: 30, 36. The British Library London/The Art Archive: 12, 17, 20, 31, 38. The British Library
London/HIP/Topfoto:front cover, 10, 25, 27, 33, 34, 35, 37. Centre Historiques des Archives Nationales Paris/Giraudon
Lauros/Bridgeman Art Library: 40. Jim Cole/Alamy: 14. Eric Lessing/AKG Images: 9. Eric Lessing/Musée Condé Chantilly/AKG
Images: 23. Musée Condé Chantilly/AKG Images: 29. Musée Condé Chantilly/Bridgeman Art Library: 26. Museo de Arte Antiga
Lisbon/Alfredo Dagli Orti/The Art Archive: 28. Museum of London/Bridgeman Art Library: 19.
Every attempt has been made to clear copyright. Should there be any inadvertent omission please apply to the publisher for rectification.

CONTENTS

A medieval lady   8

Beginnings   10

Invitation to a wedding   12

At home   14

Being a wife   16

Noble children   18

A year in the life   20

Clothes and hairstyles   22

Sports and hobbies   24

Books   26

Time to eat   28

Treating illness   30

Women who work   32

The noblest ladies   34

The lady and the nuns   36

The world outside   38

Widowhood   40

Glossary   42

Timeline/Useful websites   43

Index   44

A MEDIEVAL LADY

The medieval period of European history runs from about 1000 to 1500. This was the era of knights and their ladies. Many knights left their ladies in charge whilst they fought in a series of wars between France and England called the Hundred Years War, or went off on crusade to fight the Muslim Arab armies for control of Jerusalem. This book follows the life of a lady of the manor, and although she never existed, her tale is based on the facts we know about medieval women's lives.

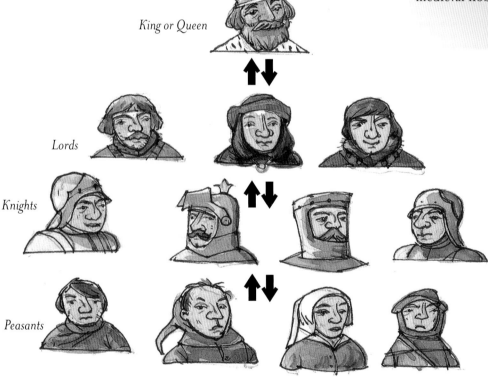

King or Queen

Lords

Knights

Peasants

Feudal society

Medieval society was made up of different classes – groups of people at different social levels. The king was at the top and he owned all the land. Next in rank came the lords, important nobles who were given big areas of land by the king in return for service, which meant fighting for him a certain number of days a year. When asked to fight by their king, they had to bring along a number of fighting men, including their knights. Knights were lesser-ranked nobles who owed fighting service to a lord. They were 'dubbed', which means they were given the rank of 'knight' in an official ceremony. A lord could grant a knight an estate, made up of some properties and land, in return for fighting a certain number of days a year. The knight then rented his land out to tenants, often peasants, in return for regular payments of money, crops or work-service.

Introducing ladies

A knight could call himself 'Sir'. The wife of a knight could use the title of 'Lady'. She would normally be the daughter of another knight, so was from a noble family herself. She would be the top-ranking female on her husband's estate – the lady of the manor. Her husband was seen as more important than her. He owned everything on his estate, and in law everything she personally owned in fact belonged to him. But she ranked second on the estate, and was his deputy. Whenever he went away to fight, she was left to manage the daily life of the estate, also called the manor.

Born a lady

Our imaginary lady of the manor is English and born in 1291, when Edward I is king. When she is 13 she marries a knight and leaves her own family's manor to go and live on his manor. It is not too far from her old home. Her new husband's family are friends of her father's, and his land is in a neighbouring area. The bride has been taught from childhood what behaviour is expected of a lady. Her parents picked her husband for her and she knew from the age of seven that she would marry him as soon as she was old enough. She was born to be a lady of the manor and has no choice.

This fine, lifelike 13th-century statue of a noble lady - Uta of Ballenstedt - is in the cathedral in Naumburg, Germany. She and her husband, the Margrave, gave money to help build the cathedral.

9

BEGINNINGS

The lady in this book is born in her parent's manor-house. Some women from the nearby village are there to help during the birth. The baby's mother has already had four children. Two have survived but another two have died young. The baby is born upstairs in the solar, the lord of the manor's private family room. Everyone prays she will be strong - on average two or three out of every ten medieval children die before the age of five, and another two or three die before reaching adulthood.

A medieval noble baby is baptised at the font by a bishop.

An urgent blessing

The baby is baptised as soon as she is born, which means she is blessed by a churchman and made a member of the Catholic Church, the only recognised religion. There is no time to lose because Church teaching insists that if she dies unbaptised, there will be no place for her in Heaven. Unbaptised babies cannot even be buried in holy ground. Once she is born and baptised, the baby's little limbs are gently massaged with a honey and salt mixture – which helps to get rid of any skin infection. Then she is swaddled, which means she is wrapped tightly in bandages, to stop her wriggling around and hurting herself and to help her limbs grow straight, so they say.

Medieval childhood

The baby grows into a little girl who spends her days playing around the manor-house and in the kitchen gardens. As she gets older her mother and her mother's female attendants teach her what

Medieval facts

The Catholic Church taught that unbaptised children went to 'limbo' when they died, a miserable place between Heaven and Hell. In an emergency a midwife was allowed to baptise a baby, if no churchman was available. Midwives can still do this today.

well-born ladies ought to know – reading, writing, manners, embroidery, singing and playing musical instruments.

When they are seven her brothers are sent away to live in the house of another knight, where they become pages and learn how to be a knight themselves. Neighbouring knights send a couple of their boys to be pages in her home, where her mother teaches them manners and her father begins to teach them what is expected of a knight.

Males come first

The little girl will not inherit her father's lands when he dies because her brothers come before her in law. But she will be given some land, called a 'dower', which she will inherit from her own mother and which she will one day pass on to her daughter. She does inherit her father's coat-of-arms, his family badge, and she can combine it with her husband's when she marries. This will make her own personal coat-of-arms which she can use on her clothing and perhaps have carved onto the wall where she lives.

If she were an only child she would inherit everything from her father. But it would be a big disaster for the family if she were an only child and her father died before she married. Then the king could take payment from anyone who wanted to be her guardian.

The future lady of the manor plays in the garden with her nurse.

The guardian could take the profits from her estate up until the day she married, and could even sell off parts of her estate.

Custody

An unfortunate widow is reminded that custody of her young children, together with her dead husband's lands, has been given to a guardian by the king. To get them back she would have to offer payment.

❖ *To Mabel, late the wife of Richard De Torpel. She must well remember that the King gave the custody of the land and heirs of the said Richard De Torpel to the Bishop of Chichester.* ❖

INVITATION TO A WEDDING

When she was seven, the young girl was betrothed to a young nobleman of 13. Neither of them had a say in the matter — it was arranged between the two families. Now she is 13 and it is time for the betrothed couple to marry. Before the 12th century they could have been married anywhere — under a tree or in a house — without the Catholic Church being involved. But now, in 1304, the church is where the marriage ceremony will take place.

Betrothal

It is six years since the betrothal ceremony took place before witnesses. If either family had chosen to break the betrothal without agreement, they could have found themselves in court. The young nobleman is 20 and has become a knight and inherited his father's estate. The young lady will bring her dowry with her into the marriage. This financial agreement between the families represents her share of her father's inheritance. Her dowry consists of some goods, money and her dower land.

Wedding day

Before the wedding, the banns are read out three times in the local church. If anybody has evidence that the planned marriage is illegal, this is when they have a chance to declare it. The bride and groom meet at the church door for the service. Here the groom announces to everyone what has been agreed as the bride's dowry, and he gives her some gold or silver and a ring, laid on a book. They make vows to each other and then go inside the church.

The noble couple meet at the door of the church to exchange vows.

Leon Battista Alberti advises Italian medieval families how to persuade their sons to marry:

❖ *Youths must be induced to take wives by persuasion, reasoning and reward.* ❖

They say prayers and then kneel under a holy cloth called a pall to have their marriage blessed. After the wedding there is a lavish feast for everyone. Once the lady is married, her property becomes her husband's for as long as he lives. He has full rights over her and by law he can even beat her if he wishes (though not too harshly).

Peasant weddings

The young lady and her friends in neighbouring manors marry young, as all nobles do. Peasant girls do things differently. They get married much later, usually in their twenties. They work as soon as they are able, and they do not marry until their grooms have some financial stability. If a peasant couple have children before they are married, the children kneel under the pall with their parents at the Nuptial (wedding) Mass, and the priest declares them legitimate – legal. After a peasant wedding, there is often a 'bride-ale', when guests bring their own food to the celebration.

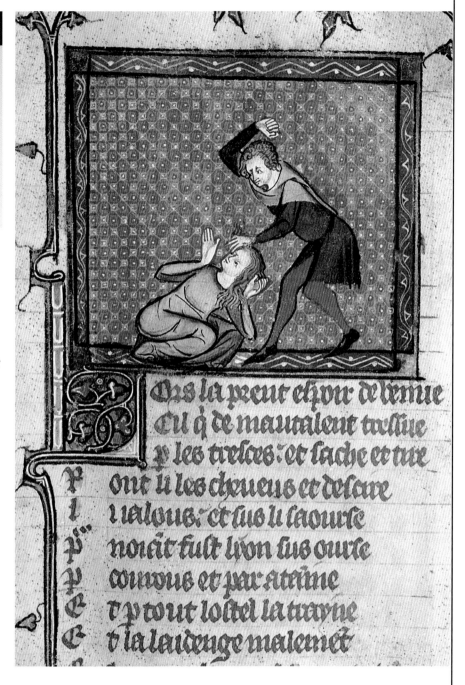

Married women had few rights in medieval times, and a husband could beat his wife.

Peasant women have to pay a sum of money to their local knight, the lord of the manor, to allow them to get married. They could be fined by the knight for having children out of wedlock.

In 1180 a lawyer highlighted a married woman's lack of rights:

❖ *Every married woman is a sort of infant.* ❖

AT HOME

After the wedding, the lady goes to live in her new home – a manor-house built with thick walls of stone surrounded by a water-filled moat. Her husband is wealthy so their shared home is large, though not as big as a castle. Only the most important nobles have those.

Outside and inside

The biggest room inside the manor-house is the Great Hall. Here everyone eats their meals and the knight and his lady meet guests. The servants who work around the manor-house all sleep in the Great Hall at night, on straw bedding. The knight and his lady are the only people with a private room, called the 'solar'. Here they have their own bed, made up with fine linen. They have bowls of water to wash in – but no lavatory. Instead there is a hole in the wall called a garderobe, with a chute beneath to direct the refuse out into the moat. Outside there is a large courtyard and outbuildings such as stables, a hen-house and a granary. The manor-house and its buildings are fortified, which means they have a high wall and a moat around them to withstand possible attacks from enemies.

The Great Hall of a manor-house was where meals were eaten and where servants slept.

14

At her needlework

Overseeing the servants

At Mass with the lord

With the gardener

Supervising the buying and storage of food (above)

Self-sufficiency

Here is a description of some of the outbuildings of a manor granted to Robert Le Moyne in 1265. It shows how self-sufficient a manor-house was, with its own livestock and barns. It also had a hen-house, dairy and granary.

❖ *Also two barns, one for wheat and one for oats. These buildings are enclosed with a moat, a wall and a hedge. Also beyond the middle gate is a good barn and a stable for cows, and another for oxen, these old and ruinous. Also beyond the outer gate is a pigsty.* ❖

Manor servants

The young lady of the manor gets to know all her servants and makes sure they do their work. As well as kitchen staff and gardeners, there are household staff who perform such duties as cleaning and lighting the fires in the rooms. It is important to keep the manor-house clean, to avoid grime and unpleasant smells. Both the lady and her husband have their own personal servants, who help dress them and look after their clothing and personal well-being.

The servants get low pay but they also get food and lodging. Most of them come from local peasant families on the estate, so they are known and trusted. They get occasional holidays when they can go to visit their families nearby.

Working in the manor

There are lots of servants to keep the manor running smoothly. There is a kitchen to run, with big fireplaces to roast meat. A young servant has the job of turning the meat on a spit over the fires until it is cooked. There are baking ovens, too. Outside there are vegetable gardens and livestock to look after.

The manor also has its own chapel where everybody goes to services led by the knight's personal priest, the chaplain. The knight's family sit in their own balcony above the servants, who worship below.

BEING A WIFE

The lady of the manor's husband is a knight and so is regularly called away for weeks at a time, to fight for his lord. She must take charge of the house and the estate while he is away. She has been taught from childhood how to manage an estate, and one day she will teach her own daughter the same responsibilities.

Advice book

Christine de Pisan, a French noblewoman living in the 14th century, wrote this in *The Book of Three Virtues*, her book of advice for women:

❖ *Because Barons and still more commonly knights and squires and gentlemen travel and go off to wars, their wives should be wise and sound administrators and manage their affairs well, because most of the time they stay at home without their husbands, who are at court or abroad.* ❖

Lady in charge

The knight employs a steward, a manager who helps to ensure the daily life of the manor runs smoothly. He keeps an account of what is spent, and makes sure there is enough food to feed everyone in the house. He also makes sure the lands on the estate are well-run. He reports problems to the knight, and if the knight is away then he reports to the lady.

The lady is ultimately responsible for making sure her servants and her family are properly fed, and she knows it is especially important to get a good harvest stored up for the winter months, when there will be much less for everyone to eat. She and the steward make sure that enough farm animals are killed to eat through the winter, preserved by smoking or salting. During the early 1300s things are especially difficult, with freezing weather and food shortages across the whole of Europe. Everyone on the estate struggles to keep themselves fed during the famine.

A lady had to plan carefully to ensure plentiful food was available at a feast.

Out on the estate

The people who live on the knight's land must give him regular rent, in money or goods, or in work-service. He employs a tax-collector called a reeve to do the job of collecting what is owed. The reeve reports to the lady when the knight is away. If somebody repeatedly fails to pay the reeve what they owe they could be turned out of their home. The lady relies on the reeve and the steward to see problems coming and advise her what to do. The estate runs as a kind of business, with money coming in and going out. When her husband is away the lady must be prepared to be the medieval version of a businesswoman.

Forced to fight

A knight's wife is expected to defend her estate if it is attacked while her husband is away. Danger is more likely to come from a hostile neighbouring knight than from a foreign invader. If ever a lady is called upon to do this, she must be prepared to quickly find weapons and organise the local people. Her husband, the knight, has trained local men to fight as best they can, mounting a defence from inside the manor-house walls using bows and arrows, clubs and axes. Occasionally medieval noblewomen might even be called upon to defend their homes from a siege lasting weeks, so they must organise not only the defence but share out the available food supply so that it lasts until the enemy gives up. This is more likely to happen if the noblewoman lives in an important castle.

There were many estate workers to be supervised when the lady's husband was absent.

NOBLE CHILDREN

T he lady of the manor married young, like her fellow noblewomen, and hopes to have as many children as possible, so that at least one will survive to inherit her husband's estate. She knows, and fears, that some of her children will die young, from illnesses untreatable in medieval times.

Praying and hoping

The lady prays to God to give her a child, and when she gives birth she prays to Saint Margaret, patron saint of childbirth. The lady even wears a 'birth girdle', a roll of parchment marked with prayers and a cross, which she thinks will help her deliver safely. Some religious houses and churches hold relics or even the Virgin Mary's own 'birth girdle', which they lend out to royalty and important aristocratic women when they are pregnant to 'help' with the birth. Just like modern women, pregnant medieval women are given medical warnings. They are warned not to drink beer, eat pork or ride on horseback in case they harm the unborn baby.

A medieval child clings to her noble mother in this manuscript painting.

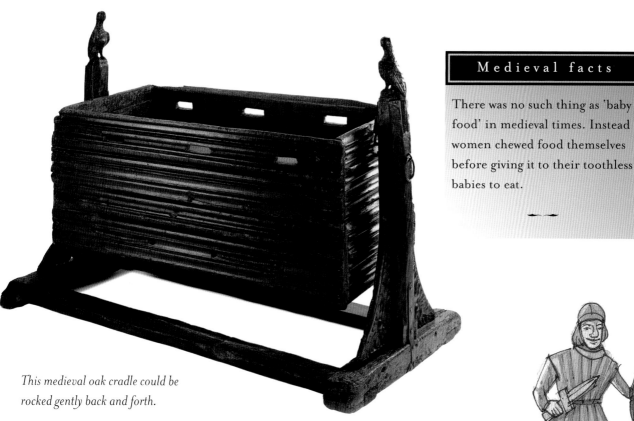

This medieval oak cradle could be rocked gently back and forth.

The lady plays at 'knights' with her son as her husband's page (attendant) stands by.

A dangerous time

The lady has a local midwife to help her, a woman with some special knowledge of childbirth. Some medieval midwives were more skilled than others, and childbirth is a common cause of death among women of the time. Mothers-to-be are advised to confess their sins to a churchman before they go into labour, so that if they die they will go to Heaven.

New mothers stay hidden at home, and only come out publicly about a month after a birth, to a special church service called a 'churching', which is meant to purify them. The new mother lights candles on the altar of Our Lady (Mary), as thanks for surviving. A churching ceremony has a party atmosphere, with all the women wearing their best clothes. If rich noblewomen have churchings, they might have fine music and a big feast afterwards.

Looking after the children

The lady teaches her children and plays games with them, too. Her attendants share the childcare. Just as her brothers did, her own sons leave when they are seven, to become pages in another knight's household. From then on she will only see them when they are given occasional holidays. She herself is in charge of two pages from someone else's family, and she teaches them manners and courtly ways. She also teaches her daughters how to be ladies. They must learn music, poetry and embroidery – all the civilised skills expected of a noblewoman.

A YEAR IN THE LIFE

The lady's daily life, and the life of all the people on her estate, varies according to the seasons, and what needs to be done to tend the land and the animals that everyone depends on to survive.

Yearly celebrations

Every year there are lots of holy days and festival days that are marked in different ways. For instance, Pentecost (Whit Sunday) is marked with a feast and then a holiday. May Day (May 1st) and Midsummer's Day (June 24th) are among the days when feasts are eaten and people celebrate and relax. At Easter the knight and his lady receive eggs from their tenants, and give the servants a special dinner. Sometimes big fairs are held in the nearby town on festival days. Here there are stalls selling goods, and there is entertainment, too, such as wrestling competitions and music. The lady sends her servants to the fairs to buy unusual items that have been brought from abroad, such as spices and silks.

Christmastide

The two weeks from Christmas Eve to Twelfth Day (January 6th) are the most important medieval

Dancers dressed in green perform in the Great Hall of a noble house at Christmastide. From a 15th-century painting.

holiday, called Christmastide. The knight gives his manor staff bonuses at this time of year, such as extra clothing and firewood. The manor-house is decorated with holly and ivy, and huge logs called yule logs are brought in to keep the fire burning through the 12 days and nights of the celebration.

On Christmas morning the lady's family goes to a service in the chapel and then there is a feast, perhaps with a fine roasted boar to eat. At the end of the meal the family tells each other riddles, and sings Christmas songs. On December 26th, called Saint Stephen's Day, the family and their attendants play games outside in the yard, such as cock-fighting and seeing who can leap the highest. Gifts are given at New Year. The lady might give her daughter an ivory comb or a ring, and her husband and sons might perhaps get fine leather belts or linen handkerchiefs, bought from the local fair and carefully stored away until Christmas.

A lady's day

On an ordinary day, the lady of the manor gets up early, soon after dawn. She puts on a piece of long underclothing called a chemise. Then she washes her face in a bowl of water put out by her attendants. She dresses, with help from her servants, and goes to the chapel with the rest of her family to say Mass. After breakfast she must attend to estate matters, if her husband is away. The main meal of the day is at about 10 or 11 am, and after that she likes to go hawking, riding and hunting with birds of prey (see page 24). After supper, she spends time in the solar, reading, sewing or talking by candlelight. Then her attendants help her to prepare for bed. They have lit a fire to keep the room warm. She washes with soap made from soda, wood ash and animal fat, though when she can get it, she buys luxury soap made abroad from olive oil and herbs. She says her prayers and goes to bed alongside her husband.

Two of the lady's favourite outdoor activities are riding (top) and hawking with her husband.

CLOTHES AND HAIRSTYLES

There are rules about who wears what type of clothing. As she is a noblewoman, the lady can wear fine clothes, studded with jewels, of the type worn by the royal court. People from lower classes are strictly discouraged from wearing anything that makes them look above their rank, and so the lower down the social ladder you are, the simpler your clothing.

Fashion victim – a lady of the French court.

A lady's clothing

The lady wears several layers of clothing. Over her chemise she wears two long tunics, one with shorter sleeves over one with long sleeves. She might wear a mantle – a short cape. Her clothes are made of wool or linen material, sometimes sent home by her husband when he is away fighting abroad. There are no ready-made clothes to purchase. She must buy lengths of material and then pay a seamstress to make her clothes. She wears a girdle (a belt that hangs down at the front), a necklace and rings, and flat shoes with pointed toes.

Hair and headdresses

When she was unmarried, the lady of the manor wore her hair without a veil. Now she is a married woman she covers her head with a veil called a wimple, that flows down the back of her head. It is secured around her face with pins, and worn with a circlet on top. Her hair is worn long underneath. Her servants sometimes redden her lips with ochre – made from powdered clay – and whiten her skin a little by dusting it with flour.

She eagerly listens to news about fashions at court, which often change, echoing new trends seen abroad. Clothing in her time is mostly coloured red, green or blue. Later on in the 14th century, plum and tan will become fashionable colours, and by the end of the century black becomes the trendiest colour for every noble.

Medieval fashion

Fashion moves fast in medieval times, usually based on the styles worn by royalty. When the lady was young, in the early 1300s, clothing was simple. Now, in the 1320s, long downward-pointing sleeves are the height of fashion, and lots of little buttons have become all the rage. Later on medieval women will wear clothes that are much more embroidered, wide wirework headdresses covered in fabric, and even tall steeple-shaped hats.

Noblemen are just as interested in fashion. One year they wear long robes, the next shorter ones. Hairstyles change too – long hair then collar-length hair, small hoods and then long pointed ones. They wear short beards, sometimes forked, and they have pointed shoes, finely decorated leather belts and jewellery.

In the *Book of the Knight of La Tour Landry*, c. 1372, a French nobleman advises his daughters against wearing make-up, and on hair-care:

❖ *Fair daughters, hold it in your heart not to put any paint or make-up on your faces which were made in God's image. Keep them as your creator and nature have ordained. Do not pluck your eyebrows or your temples or forehead. Do not wash your hair in anything but soap and water.* ❖

Fashionably dressed nobles, depicted in a Burgundian book of hours – prayer book – of the early 15th century.

The lady of the manor has time to embroider, to read and to go hawking with her own trained bird of prey. She enjoys games such as chess, which she plays with her attendants. She likes to keep a few pets – a small dog and some birds in a cage.

Servants in attendance – one holding a hawk – as the lord and lady prepare to go out.

Accomplishments

From a 13th-century poem by Robert De Blois, describing his ideal medieval heroine:

❖ *She could carry and fly a falcon, tersel and hawk,*
She knew well how to play chess and tables (backgammon),
How to read romances, tell tales and sing songs. ❖

Hawking for women

The lady goes out riding with her husband and servants, her bird of prey perched on her gloved hand. She lets it loose to catch small prey, such as rabbits. Her bird has been trained by the falconer employed by her husband, but she has spent a lot of time with it to get it used to her. Hawking has lots of social rules. Different types of people are expected to have particular species of hunting birds, and having a bird above your rank is seen as rebellious. Ladies are allowed a merlin, a breed of falcon.

Music and games

Sometimes the lady plays music (above) or sings. She enjoys a game of chess. The medieval rules are not the same as modern rules, with pieces moving slightly differently. Backgammon is very popular, too. On special occasions the household likes to play party games, such as 'hot cockles', when someone is blindfolded and struck by the other players, whom he has to identify. The lady has heard of the wealthiest people in the land playing card games, but she doesn't possess any. The cards come from

A noble couple play backgammon in this 14th-century manuscript painting.

the Middle East; they are hand-painted and very expensive.

Spinning and sewing

To while away winter evenings the lady embroiders on a frame using silks she has sent her servants to buy from a pedlar who travels from village to village, carrying his wares on a cart. She also knows how to make woollen thread, spinning it by hand using a spindle, a stick with a weight attached to it. The richer the noble, the more fine woven wool tapestries they can afford to hang on their walls. These are made by specialist weavers in town and city workshops. The lady has a fine tapestry hanging in the solar, showing hunting scenes. It helps to keep the cold out of the stone-walled room, and she loves to look at its bright colours. It is a treasure that will be passed down through the family.

BOOKS

Like many medieval ladies, the lady has her own collection of books, to help fill the time she spends in the solar. She loves books of poetry and romance, and also has a religious primer, a book of prayers for every occasion. Her favourite book is a collection of French tales of brave knights and beautiful ladies. All her books have been copied by hand and so are very precious.

Chivalry and women

In books and poetry of the time chivalry is a strong theme. The chivalrous heroes of knightly adventures worship women as pure and holy creatures, protecting them and admiring them. This tradition is called 'courtly love'. Yet at the same time, women are sometimes portrayed as untrustworthy magical creatures, evil witches disguising themselves as pretty ladies to trick knights into sin and ruin. A knight must be on the look out for these types of women and keep himself pure.

The lady and her attendants love to hear travelling minstrels, called troubadours, who occasionally arrive in her area and sing songs telling of courtly love and magical adventures.

Medieval facts

Medieval noblewomen often left their precious books to their loved ones in their wills, so we know what was in their collections. For instance, the Countess of Devon's will, made in 1390, left her daughters her primer, a book of medicine and some tales of Merlin and King Arthur.

A noble lady reading. In the medieval period bookshelves had not yet been invented. Books were kept safely in chests and then put on a stand for use.

Women writers

The lady reads her books out loud to her children and to her women friends. They are written in Norman French or in Middle English, the name for the English language used at the time. A few medieval stories and poems are written by women, such as the poet Marie de France, writing in the 12th century. In the 14th century the world's first professional woman writer, Christine de Pisan, is at work in France. Left a young widow, with three children to look after, she makes a living from writing lifestyle advice books for women and has many publishing successes.

What women learn

Noblewomen are taught how to behave from books of manners and advice. Having good manners, being religious and knowing how to run a good household is the basis of a noblewoman's education, and the books she has reflect that. But it is also generally felt that too much learning in a woman is harmful. The medieval Spanish king, Phillippe of Navarre, actually forbids women to read or write, in case they read corrupting romance stories or start writing love letters.

The Wife of Bath

In the 14th-century *Canterbury Tales* by Geoffrey Chaucer, the Wife of Bath complains that, since most medieval stories are written by men, women invariably appear the wicked ones. This version is translated into modern English.

❖ *By God, if women had but written stories,*
Like those the clergy keep in their rooms.
More would have been written of man's wickedness
Than all the sons of Adam could redress. ❖

The French author Christine de Pisan writing in her study, from a 14th-century manuscript painting.

TIME TO EAT

The lady eats better than many of the people who live on the manor because she is of noble birth. The meat, milk and crops of her husband's estate are available as food. But in famine times, when crops fail and animals die, everyone in the manor will go hungry, including the nobles.

Food at the manor

The knight and his family have three meals a day. In a good farming year there will be plenty to eat. There are vegetables and herbs from the garden, beef, pork and lamb, birds such as chickens and wildfowl, and fish from the local streams. There is milled flour to make white bread, and cheese and butter from the dairy. Everyone drinks ale or milk, as the water supply is not clean.

Animals such as wild boar, deer and rabbits live on the estate woodlands, and they are hunted for food. They are the knight's property and ordinary peasants are forbidden from hunting them. If caught they will be severely punished, perhaps by being put in the stocks.

A well-off family eats a meal in the Great Hall of their home. A linen cloth covers the table, the plates and vessels are of pewter and there is a servant to bring in the different courses.

The cook

Geoffrey Chaucer describes a cook in his *Canterbury Tales*, written in the 14th century and here translated into modern English.

❖ *They had a Cook with them who stood alone,*
For boiling chicken with a marrow-bone,
Sharp flavouring-powder and a spice for savour.
He could distinguish London ale by flavour,
And he could roast and seethe and broil and fry,
Make good thick soup and bake a tasty pie.
But what a pity — so it seemed to me,
That he should have an ulcer on his knee. ❖

Medieval facts

The medieval diet was not healthy. It was low in some important vitamins, and fruit was considered to be bad for health, the opposite of what we now know to be true. On the other hand the medieval diet was generally low in fat, unlike the diet of many wealthy people today.

A noble hunting party sets off. Game was an important source of food in medieval times.

else, for instance a cooked bird recovered with its feathers and posed so it looks alive. Small birds such as larks, thrushes and finches are eaten roasted, along with large birds such as peacocks, and even seabirds such as seagulls and cormorants. There are delicious puddings and spiced wine to drink.

Sweet and savoury tastes are often mixed together. An example is a popular dish called 'blankmanger', a kind of milky stew made from chicken paste, flour, almonds, milk and sugar or honey. At a feast exotic expensive foods from abroad might be served, such as figs, dates and oranges.

Peasant food

Most peasants on the manor do not have access to milled wheat flour, which only grows on the best land, so they make a heavy dark bread from barley and rye. After a tough harvest, they might even have to add acorns or beans to their bread recipe. The main meal is pottage, a thick soup made of any vegetables and herbs available at the time, perhaps along with oats and sometimes bacon. Everything must be preserved as well as possible, for the winter months. This is done by salting, smoking or soaking in salt water. Pigs are free to run around, eating whatever they can find, so they make an ideal cheap animal for peasants to keep through the summer and kill for winter.

A feast day

A medieval feast is a grand occasion, with many food courses and luxuries designed to show the guests how wealthy the host is. When the knight hosts a feast, he and his wife sit at the high table in the Great Hall, along with important guests. All kinds of meat and fish courses are served, along with tarts and 'subtleties', which means food disguised as something

TREATING ILLNESS

When the lady, or anyone in her family, falls ill she sends word to the local monastery for help and advice. The monks provide medical care as far as they are able, relying on their knowledge of healing herbs to produce homemade medicines they hope will help.

'Herbals' indicated which plants were medicinally useful. Shown is marigold.

All about humors

Like everyone in her time, the lady believes that the world is made up of four elements, called the 'humors'. These are fire, air, earth and water, corresponding in the body with blood, yellow bile, black bile and phlegm. Illness is thought to occur when there is too much of one or other humor in the body. Women are thought to be deficient in heat, and so are said to be weaker in mind and body. Their lack of heat is said to account for their untrustworthy nature, and they are thought to suffer from more illnesses than men. Like other women of her time, the lady must put up with some very negative attitudes towards women, both in medicine and in religion.

Medieval facts

Some medieval remedies seem inexplicable in modern times. For instance, it was thought that a good way to cure a fever was to eat a spider wrapped in a raisin, and madness was treated by hanging a bag of buttercups round the neck.

To make a plaster

Most medicines used plants. Here a medieval recipe describes how to make a plaster to be put on the skin:

❖ *Take two handfuls of mallows, one handful each of milfoil, fennel, and dwarf elder, three handfuls of leaves of leeks. Let them be cut very minutely, ground and roasted with a little water.* ❖

Religion or ritual?

In the local monastery there is a small hospital wing for very sick men. Women are cared for by other women, at the nunnery. The abbess of the local convent has a good knowledge of medicine, and there are women healers in one or two of the local villages, too. Like the monks and nuns, they use herbs and ground-up stones to create homemade cures, but they often add some ancient rituals, too, such as picking herbs when facing south at sunrise to make them stronger, and perhaps chanting an old charm as they pick. Such old healing rituals are unpopular with the Church because they smack of ancient pre-Christian beliefs, but local people still privately rely on them. The Church teaches that illness is partly due to sin, and so sick people often visit religious shrines to pray for forgiveness and thus a cure.

Bloodletting and cupping

A common treatment for illness is bloodletting, to get rid of too

much heat in the body thought to occur if someone is feverish or has an infection. A barber-surgeon, a local man who provides head-shaving, basic surgery and dentistry, is called in to cut open the patient in a way that leads to some blood loss that is not too harmful.

Another common treament is cupping. Glass cups are put on the skin to draw blood to the surface, to reduce the pressure of having 'too much blood'.

The lady uses a few herbal remedies from her own garden to cure her family of minor problems. She treats them with lemon balm for colds, marjoram for bruises, lungwort for a cough and feverfew for headaches. As she is quite wealthy she is able to buy tooth powder made from crushed seashells, and rubs it on her teeth to make them look clean. Others in her household do not clean their teeth and have mouthfuls of rotting teeth as a result.

A lady stirs medicine over the fire for her husband, who is recovering from illness.

WOMEN WHO WORK

In the local towns and villages there are peasant women who live very differently to the lady of the manor. If she meets them they treat her with great deference, knowing she is much grander than they are. They live a life of hard work, and sometimes poverty and starvation during famine times. They generally die much younger than noblewomen.

This picture of a peasant woman selling leeks is from a 1356 Italian manuscript.

A peasant wife

A peasant is someone who lives off a small piece of land, farming it and paying their local knight rent, tax or work-services for it. If they get behind on their payments, they will lose the land and be thrown out. A typical medieval peasant family is a wife, husband and two or three surviving children living in a small house along with their animals. A peasant's wife is his partner in work as well as marriage, and helps to farm the land as well as look after the family. Young peasant girls usually marry later than noblewomen because their families need them to work for a while to help make money.

Artisan women

The next step up in society from a peasant is an artisan, someone who makes a living by a trade or craft. It is possible for a single or widowed woman to become a successful artisan in her own right. If she earns enough money for herself, she can buy land of her own, run a market stall or perhaps run a shop in a local town. Eventually she might even be wealthy enough to get servants of her own. Women often work as brewers, since everyone drinks ale instead of the unclean water available. Some women make a living from practical skills such as weaving or bookbinding. There are even a few women craftworkers, such as artists. Many trades have female members, including butchers, goldsmiths and shoemakers, most of them working alongside their fathers or husbands.

The French artist Thamar (Timarete) painting a picture of Diana in about 1400.

Working for the nobles

From about the age of 12 some peasant girls might be picked to go and work in the local manor-house. They might be laundresses or dairymaids, or helpers in the kitchen. They start off on the lowliest of tasks, and gradually go up in rank, until they marry and leave the manor to run their own home. Their pay is low, but they have their food and shelter provided. Outside the manor-house, their life would probably be much tougher, especially in times of famine and disease.

THE NOBLEST LADIES

The lady of the manor does very occasionally visit the castle of her husband's lord, the nobleman who grants him his land and title. There she meets the lord's wife, who is related to royalty and so is from a much more high-born family than her own. Important aristocratic women such as this are the female celebrities of their day, setting fashions for clothing and behaviour that other women follow.

The baroness

Christine de Pisan, writing in the 14th century, gave advice to highborn women in *The Book of Three Virtues.*

❖ *These women must be highly knowledgeable about government and wise… The knowledge of a baroness must be so comprehensive that she can understand everything… Moreover she must have the courage of a man.* ❖

Queen Isabel of France enters Paris; a painting from a 14th-century manuscript.

Castle life

The life of a high-born aristocratic woman is different to a lesser-ranked lady of the manor. Her home is much larger, and there are many more servants. Her daily life involves less duties round the estate, and more leisure time for poetry-reading, hunting and music. She might entertain guests at lavish feasts and tournaments, and perhaps even play host to the king and the court. Her clothes are made of the finest materials, and her hair arranged in the latest fashion of the court. She is expected to be a patron – a financial backer and encourager – of poetry and art, and is also expected to give generously to charity. Highborn aristocratic women sometimes donate large sums of money to found new nunneries.

Ladies watch a 14th-century jousting match. Jousting was dangerous and many nobles were killed or injured.

Tournament times

Grand ladies play an important part in the ritual of tournaments – competitions between jousting knights. A lord might hold a tournament and invite knights from far and wide to take part. The lady of the manor looks forward to these rare but splendid events but hopes that her own husband will not get hurt. The noble female spectators have their own stand and give favours, such as handkerchiefs or circlets of flowers, to their favourite contestants, to wear during their jousting bouts. The lady of the castle gives out the prizes, and the winner is declared her champion. Dances are held, where the knights vie with each other to charm the women with their courtly manners.

Powerful and dangerous

High-born aristocratic women can be politically powerful, doing their best to manoeuvre their family into more power and sometimes interfering too much and getting into trouble.

The lady and her friends have been talking about the scandalous behaviour of Isabella, wife of Edward II. Neglected by her husband, she recently took her son to France where she rallied support and invaded England. She deposed her own husband and is said to have had him murdered at Berkeley Castle in Gloucestershire in 1327, so that she and her lover, Roger Mortimer, can rule on behalf of her young son.

THE LADY AND THE NUNS

I f she had not married, the lady of the manor might have considered becoming a nun, one of the few careers open to noblewomen. As it is, like all noblewomen, she is expected to give money and gifts to her local nunnery, and in return the nuns pray for her soul.

Women at the nunnery

Medieval nunneries are much smaller than monasteries, and there are less of them around the country. A nunnery might be home to 20 or 30 nuns, or even as few as ten. Their leader is called an abbess or prioress and only the daughters of nobles become nuns.

The nunnery might offer some teaching for local noble girls, in return for money. It also provides a boarding house for noblewomen who wish to stay for a while, although the Church disapproves of this. Rich noblewomen sometimes retire to a nunnery in later life, to be looked after by the nuns.

Marry - or else!

An angry Italian mother tells her daughter – who eventually became Saint Catherine of Siena – that she will not be allowed to be a nun:

❖ *Even if it breaks your heart, you will marry.* ❖

A nun uses her rosary – the string of beads – to help her pray.

Geoffrey Chaucer, here translated into modern English, introduces a nun in *The Canterbury Tales*. Her love of pets puts her amongst the less-religious nuns.

❖ *She used to weep if but she saw a mouse
Caught in a trap, if it were dead
or bleeding.
And she had little dogs she would
be feeding
With roasted flesh, or milk, or fine
white bread.
And bitterly she wept if one were dead.* ❖

A nun's life

A nun takes a vow of chastity and spends the rest of her life living in the nunnery. She wears a nun's clothing covering her head and body. Every day is a strict routine of prayer, study and work, perhaps tending the nunnery gardens or farm. There are seven religious services daily, the first one at 2 am. Then the nuns can go back to bed until 6 am, when the day properly starts. There are six more services to attend at different times until 7 or 8 pm, when the nuns go to bed.

Naughty nuns

Nuns are often criticised by churchmen. Common complaints include nuns not saying prayers properly, taking too much interest in fashionable clothes and wearing expensive jewellery, dancing, playing party games, keeping pets and even taking them into church. One story tells of a bishop who visits a nunnery and demands that the nuns' pet dogs be removed. But once the bishop has gone away the nuns whistle their dogs back. Nuns are not really meant to go outside, but they often do, even sometimes visiting monasteries.

Medieval nuns sing a religious service in the choir stalls of their convent.

Medieval facts

For most of the day nuns were expected to stay silent and communicate in sign language.

THE WORLD OUTSIDE

The lady of the manor has never travelled much outside her local area. She has certainly never been outside England. What she knows of the world comes from her books and what she has been told by her husband about his time abroad.

This 13th–century map depicts Europe, Africa and Asia. North is on the left, so the Mediterranean Sea is at the middle bottom.

Dangers on the road

Travelling is quite difficult. The roads are often badly rutted and liable to make a horse lame. Sometimes they are flooded or icy, making the way impassable. There are no signposts, and often the roads are no more than muddy tracks. There are wolves and wild boars to contend with, and also gangs of outlaws, men who have escaped from the law and now skulk in the countryside looking for travellers to rob. The lady of the manor would never think of travelling alone, and when she decides to go on a pilgrimage she takes some armed servants with her for security.

A holy pilgrimage

The lady has heard older noblewomen, especially widows, talk of their pilgrimages. She decides to make her own pilgrimage to a local shrine. It is dedicated to Mary, mother of Jesus, who is said to have appeared there in visions and caused miracle medical cures. On the journey the lady and her servants stay in nunneries and inns. When she arrives at the holy site she gives

money to help the poor and buys candles for the shrine. Like other medieval pilgrims, she is sure her journey will wipe away her sins and help her to get into Heaven.

Other more adventurous travellers go all the way to Santiago de Compostela, in Spain, the most popular medieval pilgrimage site in Europe. Here the bones of the disciple Saint James are said to rest.

When she travels, the lady rides in a litter slung between two horses.

A small world

Medieval people have little knowledge of the world outside Europe. The lady knows of France, Spain and other parts of Europe, and also of the Holy Lands because of the crusades that took place in earlier medieval times. She knows vaguely of Asia because of trade links between China and Europe, but she knows nothing of the rest of Africa, or of America or Australasia, and assumes the known world is entirely surrounded by oceans.

The lady is afraid of anyone who is not a Christian. She has been taught by the Church that all non-Christian people are enemies of the Christian Catholic kingdoms of Europe.

WIDOWHOOD

The lady of the manor's husband dies when she is 35, leaving her a widow. Widowhood is common in medieval times because of the high mortality rate. Although saddened by her husband's death, she now has more wealth and legal rights than at any other time in her life.

Free and rich

When her husband dies, all the lady's property goes back to being hers, including the dower land she brought with her on her marriage (see pages 12-13). She also gets a third of her husband's personal goods, a third going to his children and a third to the Church for the good of his soul. Her eldest son inherits the estate. Widows are supposed to be respected ladies of the community, but they also have a reputation for having a racy love-life and a love of fine living.

Problems of widowhood

In earlier times a rich noble widow could be given in marriage

This medieval wax seal belonged to a noble lady and is a strong image of a powerful and independent woman.

to whoever the king wished, unless she paid a fine to allow her to marry who she wished. This was a lucrative tax that made the king a lot of money. But the law has changed so that widows can manage their own estate, and spend their money how they like without being forced to give it to an unwanted new husband. Some widowed noblewomen choose to go to live in a nunnery, paying to be looked after there.

A medieval death

After a short illness, the lady dies in 1343 aged 52, a good age for a woman in medieval times. In her will she leaves her books to her daughter, who also inherits her dower land, and she leaves some of her possessions to her favourite tenants and servants. She chooses to be buried next to her husband in the local church, and she has already had an effigy – a brightly-painted carving – made of her lying beside the effigy of her husband. His effigy shows him in full armour – her carving shows her in a fashionable gown of the time. After a grand funeral, the lady is laid to rest beside her husband.

The Black Death

Sweeping across Europe in 1348/49, the disease known as the 'Black Death' – thought to be plague – killed one-third of the population. By dying in 1343, our lady of the manor has escaped the horrors of the dreadful disease that spared neither men, women nor children.

A noble lady's grave is marked by a stone effigy - such as this one - in the local parish church. The paint has worn off.

GLOSSARY

Abbess ❖ the head of a religious community of nuns

Alms ❖ money given to charity

Artisan ❖ a craftsperson, who makes a living from a skill such as candle-making, weaving and so on

Banns ❖ a wedding announcement that must be read out on three separate occasions in a church before a wedding can take place

Baptise ❖ to pronounce a baby a member of the Christian Church – it was said unbaptised people could not go to Heaven

Betrothal ❖ a marriage arrangement, when young people are promised to each other in marriage. In medieval times a noble woman had no choice in whom she married

Black Death ❖ the name given to the plague that ravaged Europe in the late 1340s

Bloodletting ❖ cutting open someone to allow blood to flow out

Catholic ❖ the religion of all Europe in medieval times, headed by the Pope

Chaplain ❖ a personal priest, who provides religious instruction and services for a noble family

Chemise ❖ a lady's under-petticoat, rather like a simple nightie

Chivalry ❖ a code of honourable behaviour that knights were meant to follow

Churching ❖ a special church service held to purify a medieval woman after she has given birth

Coat-of-arms ❖ the official badge of a noble family

Courtly love ❖ the pure and chivalrous admiration of women, as set out in medieval poems and stories of brave knights

Cupping ❖ cups put on the skin to draw blood to the surface

Disciple ❖ one of the 12 closest followers of Jesus Christ

Dower land ❖ land given to a bride by her family when she marries

Dowry ❖ money and goods given to the groom by a bride's family when she marries

Estate ❖ land and properties owned by a nobleman

Famine ❖ mass starvation caused when crops fail

Garderobe ❖ a medieval toilet – a hole in the wall with a chute leading outside

Girdle ❖ a belt worn by a medieval woman, with its ends hanging down at the front

Great Hall ❖ the large main room in a castle or manor, where meetings were held and meals eaten

Hawking ❖ hunting with birds of prey (now called falconry)

Heir ❖ someone who is first in line to get land, goods, and perhaps a noble title passed down to them on their parents' death

Humors ❖ elements thought to be in the body, corresponding to fire, earth, air and water

Inheritance ❖ land, money and sometimes a noble title handed on by a relative when they die. In medieval times the oldest son was always first in line to inherit everything

Joust ❖ a tournament where two knights rode towards each other and scored points by striking their opponent with a lance

Knight ❖ a lesser-ranked noble who owes allegiance (loyalty) to a lord

Limbo ❖ a miserable place where unbaptised babies were said to go, between Heaven and Hell

Lord ❖ a highly-ranked nobleman

Manor-house ❖ a nobleman's home, smaller than a castle

Mantle ❖ a short cloak

Medieval ❖ the period of history roughly between 1000 and 1500

Merlin ❖ a type of small hawk used by medieval ladies for hunting

Middle English ❖ a medieval form of the English language

Monastery ❖ a religious community of monks

Norman ❖ something or someone connected to the French forces that invaded England in 1066, led by William the Conqueror from Normandy. For instance, a castle described as 'Norman' means it was built by the invaders

Nunnery ❖ a religious community of nuns

Our Lady ❖ the Virgin Mary, mother of Jesus

Pagan ❖ pre-Christian religion and rituals

Page ❖ a young boy aged seven or more, who served a knight and his family, while learning to be a knight

Patron ❖ a financial backer

Peasant ❖ a poor person with no rank, who makes a living farming land belonging to a noble

Pilgrimage ❖ a trip to a holy shrine

Pottage ❖ a thick soup made from vegetables

Primer ❖ a book of prayers

Reeve ❖ a knight's tax-collector

Shrine ❖ a holy site, visited by pilgrims

Steward ❖ a knight's household assistant, who helped him manage his estate

Solar ❖ a private family room above the Great Hall

Tapestry ❖ a decorative woven wall-hanging

Tenant ❖ someone who rents land or property belonging to somebody else

Wimple ❖ a veil worn off the face, draped down the back of the head

Work-service ❖ days of labour given to a lord as a form of rent

Yule log ❖ a giant log that burns throughout Christmastide

TIMELINE

Useful medieval history websites

www.fordham.edu/halsall/sbook.html

A website where you can read many original documents.

www.trytel.com

A website that provides historical information about cities and towns during the medieval period and much original source material through its Florilegium Urbanum.

www.oxfordshirepast.net

For local source material, visit this website.

www.the-orb.net

The website for the On-Line Reference Book for Medieval Studies.

www.mnsu.edu/emuseum/history/middleages/

A website where you can focus on life as a medieval peasant, knight, nun or merchant.

For more detail visit:
www.pitt.edu
www.history.ac.uk

c.1000	over the next 200 years the European population grows enormously
c.1000	a heavier wheeled plough, which cuts deeper, replaces the lighter 'hook' plough across Europe – more use of horses in farming
1066	William of Normandy invades England – and is crowned King
1096	the crusades begin – religious wars in the Middle East
c.1100	over the next 200 years, there is a great expansion of peasant settlement in Europe
c.1100	gradual introduction of the 'three-field' agricultural system across much of northern Europe
1135-54	civil war in England
1150	knights start to use coats-of-arms
1146–1254	further crusades - 2nd to 7th
c.1190	first windmills in Europe
c.1200	some peasant houses are being built of stone in northern Europe
c.1200	German peasant houses begin to introduce a smokeless stove (stube) to heat their homes
c.1200	horses replace cattle to pull heavy loads in northern European
c.1200	money rents gradually replace labour services – growth of towns, trade and the money economy
1205	the River Thames freezes and can be crossed over the ice
1207	the Order of St Francis is formed in Italy
1208	King John quarrels with the Pope, who bans church services in England
1215	King John signs the Magna Carta, giving nobles more power
1252	Henry III is given a polar bear, which swims in the River Thames with a muzzle and chain
1260	the cathedral is consecrated at Chartres in France
1265	Marco Polo travels to the Far East
c 1270	the oldest paper manufacturing in Christian Europe at Fabriano, Italy
1279	new silver coins created in England – the groat (4d), round farthing and halfpenny
1285	spectacles are made in northern Italy
c 1310	the mechanical clock is perfected
1317	heavy rains and ruined harvests cause famine across Europe
1323–28	peasant revolts in the Netherlands
1337	the outbreak of the Hundred Years War between England and France
1344	the first English gold coin, the noble, is worth 6s 8d
1346	Battle of Crécy – the French are defeated
1348–49	the arrival of the bubonic plague, 'Black Death', in Europe
1361	plague breaks out again
1362	William Langland begins to write his poem, 'Piers Plowman'
1369	harvests fail across Europe
1381	the Peasants' Revolt in England
1387	Chaucer begins his *Canterbury Tales*
1388	the first town sanitation act is passed in the English parliament
1437–38	ruined harvests, famine and plague occur in many parts of Europe
1438–40	heavy rains and ruined harvests in England
1430–70	economic crises hit England – many peasants are ruined
1453	Hundred Years War ends
1470	an economic revival begins
1500	knights no longer go to war – their main role is to be a landowner

INDEX

A

aristocrats 18, 34-35
artisans 32, 33, 42
artists 32, 33

B

banns, wedding 12, 42
baptism 10, 42
betrothal 12, 42
birds (of prey) 21, 24, 42
Black Death 41, 42, 43
bloodletting 31, 42
books 26-27, 38

C

Canterbury Tales, The 27, 28, 37, 43
castles 14, 17, 34, 35, 42
Chaucer, Geoffrey 27, 28, 37, 43
childbirth 10, 18, 19
children 10, 16, 18-19, 29
chivalry, code of 26, 42
Christmastide 20, 21, 42
church 12, 18, 19, 37, 41, 42
Church 10, 12, 31, 36, 39, 40, 42
churching 19, 42
clothing 11, 15, 19, 21, 22-23, 34,
        37, 41, 42
coat-of-arms 11, 42, 43
court, royal 16, 22, 34
craftworkers 32, 33, 42
crusades 8, 39, 43
cupping 31, 42
custody 11

D

de Pisan, Christine 16, 27, 33, 34
diet, medieval 28-29
dower 11, 12, 40, 41, 42
dowry 12, 42

E

education 11, 19, 27, 36
Edward I 9
Edward II 35
Eleanor of Aquitaine 35

embroidery 11, 15, 19, 21, 24, 25
estate, the 9, 11, 12, 15, 16, 17, 18, 20, 21,
        28, 34, 40, 41, 42

F

famine 16, 28, 32, 33, 42, 43
farming 28-29, 32, 42, 43
fashion 22-23, 34
feasts 13, 16, 19, 20, 21, 29, 34
festivals 20-21
feudalism 8-9

G/H/I

games 19, 24, 25
garderobe 14, 42
Great Hall 14, 20, 28, 29, 42
hairstyles 22, 23, 34
hawking 21, 24, 42
herbs 21, 28, 29, 30, 31
hobbies 24
holidays 15, 19, 20-21
Holy Lands 39, 42
humors 30, 42
Hundred Years War 8, 43
hunting 21, 25, 28, 29, 34, 42
illness 18, 30-31, 41
inheritance 11, 12, 18, 40, 41, 42

J/K/L

jousts 35, 42
kings 8, 9, 11, 34, 35, 41, 43
knights 8-17, 19, 26, 28, 29, 32, 35, 42, 43
ladies, aristocratic 18, 34-35
lady of the manor,
        birth 10-11
        childhood 10-11
        children 18-19, 27
        daily life 14-21
        death 41
        education 11, 27
        funeral 41
        leisure 20-21, 24-25
        marriage 9, 12-13, 14, 40
        running the estate 15, 16-17
        widowhood 40-41

M

make-up 22, 23
manners 11, 19, 27, 35
manor-house 10, 14-15, 17, 21, 33, 42
map 38
Mass 13, 15, 21
medicine 26, 30-31
midwives 10, 19
minstrels 26
monasteries 30, 31, 36, 37, 42
music 11, 19, 20, 24, 26, 34, 37

N/P

nunneries 31, 34, 36-37, 39, 41, 42
nuns 31, 36-37, 42
pages 11, 19, 42
patrons 34, 42
peasants 8, 9, 13, 15, 28, 29, 32-33, 42, 43
pilgrimage 39, 42
priests 13, 15, 42
primers 26, 42

R

reading 11, 21, 24, 26-27, 34
reeves 16, 42
remedies 30-31
rights, women's 9, 13, 33, 40

S

servants 14, 15, 16, 20, 21, 22, 24, 25, 28,
        34, 35, 39, 41
shrines 31, 39, 42
solar 10, 14, 21, 25, 26, 42
sports 20, 21, 24-25, 35, 42
stewards 16, 42

T/W

tournaments, jousting 34, 35, 42
travel 38-39
wars 8, 16, 43
weaving 25, 32, 42
weddings 12-13
widows 11, 27, 32, 39, 40-41
William the Conqueror 8, 42, 43
women, working 32-33

These are the lists of contents for each title in *Medieval Lives*:

Peasant

Introduction · First years · Peasant cottage · Childhood
The Church · Marriage · Land · Work-service for the manor · The manorial court
The working year · Feeding the family · Sickness and health · Women's work · Earning money
Games and entertainment · Freedom · Last days · Glossary · Timeline/Useful websites · Index

Merchant

Introduction · First days · House and home · Growing up · School · Becoming a merchant
Marriage · The wool trade · Travel and communication · War and piracy · Secrets of success
Branching out · Wealth and property · The merchant's wife · Good works · Health and diet
The end · Glossary · Timeline/Useful websites · Index

Knight

All about knights · A future knight is born · Time to leave home · Becoming a squire
A squire goes forth · Becoming a knight · Invitation to the castle · Joust! · Called to war
Battlefield tactics · Dressed to kill · Weapons · Siege warfare · Pilgrimage · Returning home
Knightly duties · Death of a knight · Glossary · Timeline/Useful websites · Index

Nun

Introduction · Birth · Childhood and education · To the nunnery – postulant
The nunnery itself · Taking the veil – novice · Daily life – the offices · The inner life
Daily routine · Enclosure · Cellaress and librarian · The world outside · Priests and nuns
Poverty and personal possessions · A visitation · Difficult times · Death · Glossary
Timeline/Useful websites · Index

Lady of the Manor

A medieval lady · A lady is born · Invitation to a wedding
At home with a lady · Wifely duties · Noble children · A year in the life
Clothes and hairstyles · A lady's hobbies · A lady's books · Time to eat · The lady falls ill
Women who work · The noblest ladies · A visit to a nunnery · The world outside
Widowhood · Glossary · Timeline/Useful websites · Index

Stonemason

Introduction · Birth · Childhood and growing up · Training - the quarry
Training - the building site · Rough-mason – a bridge · Summoned to work - a castle
A real 'mason' - the abbey · A growing reputation · Stone-carver · The lodge
Under-mason for the college · Master-mason for the cathedral · Designing the cathedral
Building the cathedral · Retirement · End of a life · Glossary · Timeline/Useful websites · Index